Tropical Blessings

A World War II True Story of

Survival, Endurance, and Love

by Betty Silberstein
betty@silber.com.br

© 2015

Preface

There are moments in life that are absolutely crucial; moments that mark a turning point and print a new course to the history of an individual, of a nation: they are "stellar moments" – in the words immortalized by Stefan Zweig, Austrian author, rooted in Brazil. This is the story of one of these stellar moments; although it did not mark the history of a nation, it was crucial for a man – also another Austrian – who rebuilt his life in Brazil. Thanks to him, future generations will be able to retell this incredible narrative.

My grandfather, August Silberstein, was a well-established pharmacist in the city of Vienna, Austria. He had a natural endowment for public relations and a perfect pitch. He enjoyed being with people, was known in the neighborhood and well-liked by his warmth and kindness. Lover of good music, his house was frequented by the best musicians of the time, who couldn't refuse to accept his friendship. And as can be noted by his surname, he was Jewish.

One day, in 1938, August was caught in a German SS raid. These raids were becoming increasingly frequent and the negative consequences for the Jews arrested were starting to get more and more noticed by the population.

The protocol was methodical, practical and direct; in short: very Germanic. People were inspected, their documents scrutinized. They would be arrested or released as appropriate. Their freedom depended simply on having the right paperwork. In this case, August's luck was having an Italian driver's license in his pocket.

When prey and predator face – and both are not animals but men – mere survival instinct does not explain the outcome of events. Other authentically human factors such as ingenuity, creativity, and cunning play a decisive role. Philosophers could debate during an entire lifespan on the problem of how to achieve true freedom. In this case, achieving it required a simple decision that had to be made in a split second. The chosen strategy was to pretend to be an Italian, which language August knew perfectly. A simple solution, such as most solutions to life's major problems, but not without risks.

The police officer, in a rush to fulfill his duty and contribute to ethnic cleansing, could not release any "bad" element. In fact, a quick observation would lead the officer to suspect that my grandfather's face could betray a Semitic origin. However, mere suspicion was not enough, and the officer tried by all means to find out if the alien was or was not a phony. August stuck to the strategy of being Italian; his sweaty hands gripped the Italian driver's license tensely, with the same force with which the castaway embraces the floating board. The predator does not let the prey escape easily, and tries to exhaust all his resources. Questions and cross-checks were constantly delivered as a burst of gunfire. Every question was answered in perfect Italian repeating he understood nothing; that he was from Italy, to where he wanted to return as soon as possible.

Finally, the SS officer told him, in loud German:

"You may go. You are just another dumb Italian"

The predator was waiting for the reaction of its prey. In this split second, which for my grandfather probably seemed torturing hours, such a tense silence followed, that my grandfather could practically listen to his own sweat pouring down his neck. And thus the supreme moment, the moment of unerring response when life smiles, the heavens open and the world lights up with new colors. August's response was no response, he remained perfectly still, did not move a muscle, until the inquiring officer shoved him away, signaling with his hands that he could go.

Free. This was what he eagerly expected to hear. It was the perfect scenario imagined and it became reality. The freedom, the yearning of every heart, was available to him. Every fiber of his being urged him to run away through all these people and flee. However, he started walking slowly. Never has such a narrow path among so many people seem appropriate as a symbol of hope.

The square where all this happened was full of people, some of them clients or acquaintances to the friendly young pharmacist, who has not gone unnoticed. And as the caution is not characteristic of emotionally inflamed masses, there were many unnerving references to him:

"There goes our August!" – A neighbor shouted scared.

"Herr Silberstein!" – called another, also concerned with the best intentions.

With a slight nod, a slight head turn denouncing his attempt to pass by, my grandfather had the presence of mind to ignore his name, to ignore some people he knew, to ignore the noise of the crowd and finally walked on as if he did not know any of them.

An inner silence shielded him of all external agitation. His face, daring on the outside, disguised a bubbly adrenaline within, exploding together with new and unsettled thoughts. With his heart racing, endearing scenes of his past life passed through his mind. With equal force, scenes of his near future. How would it all end? The projection of scenarios seethed: how long could he keep pretending he was Italian? If revealing his true identity, what would become of him, of his mother? Where could they go? What could he do? And amid this swirl of thoughts about past and future, a reality check: the present life, the one before them, and the one they were experiencing.

From this supreme moment on, when August Silberstein decided what to do in the middle of the chaos that was overcoming over Europe, the basis of this story will begin.

Augusto Castejón Lattaro Silberstein

From the Author

People might ask me why I wrote this.

That's quite simple: because my in-law's life is a story that needs to be told, not only to their descendants (which are also mine) but to the whole world.

I felt a little like playing "Sherlock Holmes" for a good part of the story. I did have some real facts (bits and pieces lightly told to us here and there by my in-laws, our aunt – Tante Anni – plus one of my mother-in-law's best friend Eva Todor, but not nearly enough to make out the whole puzzle).

I also found very few photos from that time, some letters and writings (handwritten in German and Hungarian, something that did not make my task any easier).

In spite of the lack of information, I think I managed to retell pretty much close to the truth the story of these people that were so important to us, their family.

My son Guto (named after his grand-father) did a wonderful job on writing a superb preface. I would like to thank him very much for doing it and for revising the book as I wrote it.

It was an honor for me to be able to put together pieces of the life of some very special people that belonged to a generation that actually lived in a painfully intimate way those sad facts that today turned out into history. And history should not be forgotten!

Betty Silberstein

Prologue

August Silberstein was a well-established pharmacist in Vienna. He was caught in a German SS raid: people were inspected, documents scrutinized. His face plus the surname betrayed a Semitic origin. He could certainly be arrested by this "high" offense. His freedom depended simply on having the right paperwork. In this case, August's luck was having an Italian driver's license in his pocket, besides speaking fluent Italian. With this little trick, the officer finally signaled with his hands that he could go.

Afraid of how long he could keep pretending he was Italian, of what would become of him, of his mother, and of his fiancée, August Silberstein decided right there what to do in the middle of the chaos that was smothering Europe.

Chapter One

It was like any other morning: the pharmacist left his family's well-known and highly regarded Pharmacy, in the heart of the city.

August waved his mother goodbye as she looked at him through one of the first-floor residence windows.

Looking at her placid face, no one would notice the many worries Frau Clothilde Silberstein carried in her heart.

Since her husband died, her only concern was geared to her now grown up kids.

Gertrude, her daughter, married to a lawyer, Oskar Faber.

They had a beautiful little girl and lived in France: her son-in-law swore it was the safest place in the world and an area Hitler would not dare to invade. After all, he told her, Paris is a city which is practically synonymous with *l'amour* with couples strolling, holding hands beside the Seine! It was unthinkable to accept the fact that anything so horrendous like a war would disturb the place! Clothilde had her doubts…

After the death of her husband her only son took over the Pharmacy. He wanted to be a doctor and had been doing very well until the 3rd year of Medicine School. However, in 1935, not to taint Aryan blood, Hitler's *Nuremberg Decrees* stroke full force with its anti-Semitic laws. August had to quit Medicine School (from then on forbidden for Jews), taking a course he was still allowed: Biochemistry. Luckily, he finished it before Jews could no longer attend German and Austrian universities at all. Now he was a Pharmacist, following his father's steps.

A few weeks earlier, her son, so full of energy and zest for life, announced he was going to get engaged. She was very skeptical about this, because so far the young man had shown no incline whatsoever to get married. She wondered when (and if) the wedding would take place in the middle of such uncertain times.

In the beginning of October, the Silbersteins had to sell their Pharmacy to non-Jews. As soon as the paper work of the transaction was ready, they would have to stop working in it for good. What would they do to keep the kind of business they were used to run?

Gustl (as he had been called by his family since he was born) made his way through the courtyard. He stopped at the iron-wrought gate and pulled a packet of cigarettes out of the breast pocket of his immaculate tailor-made double-breasted suit.

Clothilde Silberstein smiled to herself, remembering decades ago when she and her husband used to go to fun costume parties. The last one they attended to, she dressed herself as a "cigarette": a simple long sleeveless straight white gown. Instead of the usual beads or fringe covering the entire dress – the fashion then – she had hung dozens of cigarettes all over the dress, which the awe-struck guests were allowed to pick as she strode around the ball room. Emile, her elegant husband, chic in his tuxedo, enjoyed himself immensely at his wife's wit. Amusement flickered in her eyes and one corner of her mouth lifted, while she remembered yet another funny event in the past.

Whenever the family travelled together by train to their villa in Italy to spend the winter months, avoiding the Viennese dreadful winter, they would take a first class cabin. However, six people could fit in that cabin, so they devised a way to keep "intruders" out: they glued enormous and hideous false warts in awkward places in their faces, with a few warts sticking ones out of their noses, just for good measure! Of course every single passenger who dared open that particular cabin door would close it immediately and add a hasty "sorry". This way, they had the whole area only for themselves. How happy those times were…

Gustl lit his cigarette, closed the gate behind him and waved his mother goodbye.

Chapter Two

That morning, August ran his errands and was finally ready to get back home. He still had the whole afternoon ahead of him to attend other clients in the Pharmacy.

He finally got to the Square close to their house. He stopped dead still. A crowd filled the Square: a very quiet crowd, positioned in lines. SS policemen and their vile looking dogs kept everyone in place for inspection.

It was too late for him to turn back and run away. Some guard had already seen him and beckoned to him with a rifle to stand at the long queue where SS policemen were asking for documents.

A guard's harsh, resonant voice stopped him in his tracks. A tall young SS officer, dressed in an aggressive black uniform, came to him for inspection. A feeling of danger inexplicably bubbled up. His heart began to beat faster. August shuddered as he watched the man's mouth twist into a sort of snarl and could feel an inexplicable hate in his inquisitor's eyes. The officer stretched out his arm in a stiff Nazi salute and ordered:

"Documents!"

Quickly, the young Austrian acted on impulse, probably inherited from the constant pranks his parents used to play.

"*Io non parlo Tedesco!*" – He answered, and showed to the controller his Italian driver's license, something he always carried with him.

He avoided looking into the German soldier's eyes, fixing his own stare into his gleaming boots.

"Show me your documents!" – The officer's face contorted into a mask, his cheeks darkening with rage, after the continued failed attempts of questioning.

The pharmacist feigned not to understand a word of what was being asked. Then, he heard the officer saying, concealing his disappointment, dismissing him with the hand, smiling cynically:

"Just another dumb Italian. You may go!"

Gustl heard the policeman click his heels as he punctiliously dismissed him. He stuck his literally life-saver Italian driver's license back into his pocket, bent his head and walked briskly away through the Square.

It was colder than when he left in the morning; but, probably, he felt colder than he should because of the enormity of what had just happened. He raised his collar mechanically. His mind was completely taken up by the implications of what he had experienced. He has not been totally satisfied by his actions. His bravado could have easily been blown by any remark made from some of his acquaintances standing in that line. He had to do better next time!

After this experience, Gustl firmly believed that leaving their country would be the only way to be well out of reach of Nazi restrictive policies against the Jews.

His mind was in turmoil, in a whirl. He could see nothing clearly, except deciding then and there:

"There won't be a next time. Tonight I have to make up my mind and decide what we are going to do."

What he did not know was that that same night would be one the world would never forget: *Kristallnacht*, "The Night of Broken

Glass", November, 9th, 1938, All over Germany, Austria and other Nazi controlled areas, Nazi storm troopers with members of the *SS* and Hitler Youth beat and murdered Jews, broke into and wrecked Jewish homes and shops, which had their windows smashed and contents destroyed. Mob violence broke out as the regular German police stood by and crowds of spectators watched.

Chapter Three

Gustl was shaking so badly that he barely managed to unlock the back door of his house. He did not even touch the mezuzah placed high on the doorframe.

"Mother! Mother!"

Clothilde Silberstein waddled forward into the hall with its fine Persian rugs, the elegant furniture that included a particularly cute small table with innumerable fragile knick-knacks. She had a dreadful feeling her son was about to reveal some tragedy.

"Thank God you arrived. I saw so many people gathered at the Square and was afraid for you. What happened?"

The son hastily explained what happened. And what were the options awaiting them.

The old woman couldn't believe what she heard.

"But, Gustl, to leave behind everything we worked for our whole lives? Ever since taking over your father's business, you have put in the time and effort required to make our Pharmacy respected all over Vienna. How will we live? Shall we go to France, to your sister's?"

"No, Mother," – he said in a resigned, and quite unlike him, worn-out voice – "from now on definitely Europe is NOT a place for us. Not for me. Not for you. Not for any Jews! Since the *Anschluss* we've been having a harder and harder time."

"But where will we go to?"

"We're in great danger! I scarcely need to tell the disposition of Hitler's force. He wants to eliminate Austrian Jewry from economic life, to deprive us of all our financial resources, and to compel us to leave the country without means. Remember a few months ago, on April when we had to sign a paper stating we were Jews? Last month we had to sell our Pharmacy to a non-Jew named Herr Zister. The 61 thousand Reichsmark he paid us were not near enough the real price of it, but at least, now, we'll put this money into good use: saving our lives. The situation in Vienna right now is characterized by confusion, uncertainty and a state of instability."

Clotilde still felt vividly the post *First World War* menace that hung over everybody's life. It was difficult to describe the dreadful feeling that crept in her bones when she remembered a war-torn and distraught city, where the apparatus of war was visible, audible, with sandbags, road blocks, boarded-up shops, the sudden diminishing lights as power failed or was reduced, the distant drone of aircraft, the clatter of military vehicles and the voices of their crews, as they made their way through distant venues of engagement.

After three years of merciless warfare, almost all the shops in town were shabby and neglected, with grimy windows half concealing what little merchandise the shopkeepers had for sale. It was a pathetic attempt at recapturing the stylishness and luxury of pre-war days.

She was so intensely feeling all these memories that she gave a start when her son added in a bitter undertone:

"I'll try to get us to Central America. There is a promising life there for us."

"What? Where?"

"I have been thinking about that for some time. A friend told me that we can live quite well over there. We must be optimist, Mother! We don't really have many choices!" – Outwardly, Glustl managed to retain his composure, but inwardly he crumpled, a mass of conflicting emotions.

"And what about your fiancée?"

"I will contact her later, after everything is decided."

She heard the concern in her son's voice. The mere idea to go to a tropical unknown land, maybe live in a jungle – who knew? – turned her lips dry and the palms of her hands sweaty. She was feeling discouraged; there was no hope left of changing the situation. Such a fate! She felt defeated. Every other thought flew momentarily out of her mind.

Chapter Four

In hushed tones, the never-ending discussion between mother and son went on and on through the whole night and early morning.

While talking, the young man went from one room to the other, sorting out what he could take with them to provide for some living during a certain length of time. All their main belongings - money that had been hidden, clothes, jewels, etc. - had been tipped in the middle of the living room to be sorted out and arranged in the suitcases: the debris of their lives.

Clothilde Silberstein leaned back on a soft and old arm-chair, her favorite. Clutching a handkerchief in her hands, her eyes drifted around the room, her mind a blur. She was sixty-one years old. How can one this old restart life from scratch?

Picking up his *yarmulke,* the Jew's embroidered skullcap, the young pharmacist thought he probably wouldn't be able to use it anymore; however, he tuck it in the middle of the clothes he was arranging. It was not wise to walk around with it in his pocket.

He packed the one allowed suitcase for himself and snapped it shut. Then he neatly arranged a pile of things to put into his mother's suitcase, although she kept refusing to go with him. He glanced at the elegant living-room, the valuable bronze and ivory sculptures, the pictures, the furniture, his beloved piano... all must be left behind.

With its worldwide reputation as a city of music, Vienna's first-class orchestras and ensembles gave the city its seal of excellence. August was a regular visitor of the *Opera*. Things – he sadly realized – that were only going to be part of his life's history, because living in Central America he would be lucky enough if he did not have to share a house with snakes and other hideous tropical "delights"…

While methodically sorting out things, he kept thinking he had to get some papers for them. The best bet would be to get them in Italy. He would go by himself, get the permits and then he would pick up his mother. Together, they would go wherever destiny would take them. He wasn't sure when this was going to happen, but decided to pack her suitcase anyway. Even if she would undo it later…

His fiancée? Well, he would deal with that later. Probably much later…

He looked at the clock. It was half past four AM. He took a quick bath, shaved and put fresh clothes on before leaving.

He shuffled to the living-room, filled a glass with cognac and sat for a few moments at the dining-room table. The feeble light twinkled on the facets of the crystal and the amber liquid. He drummed his fingers on the table and turned his head with a startled movement towards the window: the instinctive fear of a man being pursued! He shook his head as if clearing the feeling. Leaning forward, staring at the piano, he propped his arms on his knees, smiling absently at the empty glass as he rolled in in his hands. He wondered, sadly, if he'd ever have any other happy *soirées* with his friends.

He shivered, noting, prosaically, that his stomach was rumbling with hunger. He went to the kitchen and ate something. There was no more reason for postponing his leave. He was ready to go. He did not want to risk any delays.

When he faced his mother, he saw there was darkness in her eyes that robbed them of their old penetrating brightness. He only hoped she would be able to stand the strain.

"Do you realize, Gustl, that we might never come back to this city, to our country, to this house, our home?" – She choked on the words.

"Indeed I do, Mom. And I doubt if Austria will continue to be our home. There is no longer a future for us here."

Both were crying. They stayed embraced for a long time, one – unsuccessfully – wanting to comfort and give strength to the other. Finally they parted.

He took a last look around, grabbed his coat and his hat, picked up his suitcase and left, closing the door of his home and his life behind him. The prospect of war was nothing compared with the struggle to overcome the heartache of not being able to keep contact with his own country, his own life.

Chapter Five

He hobbled downstairs and flew out of the house. This time, he did not turn back to wave his mother good-bye. He was afraid he wouldn't have the guts to proceed with the fleeing plans.

He strode briskly through the gate, which he did not care to close afterwards, towards the uncertain future that awaited him.

He passed by the conservatory where he studied piano; it had been closed to become sub-offices of some government department. The ancient building brooded through the murk of rain.

As he walked quickly through the well-known streets where he had grown up and lived all his life, completely absorbed in his thoughts and worries, it took a while to realize the noises that grew in volume as he withdrew from his home. That's when he became more and more horrified at what he saw: members of the Nazi party were joined by civilians, forming mobs that torched shops and synagogues. The fire department personnel intervened only when the blaze threatened neighboring buildings.

It didn't take long for him to understand the situation. What he witnessed was a massive, coordinated brutal attack on Jews. Jewish businesses were vandalized and ransacked.

He knew then that he could not leave his mother for later. He had to go get her now and leave the country immediately. He was scared stiff and couldn't take it out of his head that he was escaping from his own compatriots! The irony of it!

To get exit visas and other documentation necessary for emigration he would be required to stand in long lines, night and day, besides paying an exit fee. He had a better idea than go through all that. Even so, he felt small and hopeless walking by the shade of the grey buildings. The rain hit him like a slap across the face.

He lengthened his stride and got back home as fast as he could. Under high protests, he got his mother to follow him to an unknown future. Quite shocked, the frightened Clothilde still insisted on packing some bread and cold cuts that would be handy at least during the first part of their journey. They locked the house and left, without knowing that, moments afterwards, a heavy boot landed one savage kick on the bottom panel of the front door. It cracked, but it did not split open. After much banging and swearing, the burly figures of the two men carrying guns disappeared through the stairs and then into the street: the dreaded German Gestapo, notorious throughout Europe for their almost fanatical love of brutality.

At that precise moment, the Silbersteins were a couple of blocks away from their home.

Unquestionably the blitz at the Square that so terrified August was what saved his and his mother's lives.

Dawn was breaking when they were nearing the train station.

Chapter Six

Gustl had some friends in Arnoldstein, a quiet little town 237 miles from Vienna, in the southeastern Alps. It conveniently bordered Italy. From there, he would devise a way to leave Europe.

He got their tickets and although trains were running in a sketchy sort of way, in less than two hours they were heading to the first part of their trip.

From the moment his mother knew where they were going, she was less apprehensive. The thought of being with nice friends cheered her; a little of the sadness evaporated. With slightly higher spirits, they settled in the train cabin, refusing to think of the following steps they would have to take.

The train was not so crowded, but it ran quite slowly and stopped more often than the travelers would like it to. The "chuck-chuck" plus the tiredness and the strain of the last hours lulled them to a merciful sleep. Finally, in the middle of the afternoon, the train jolted to a definite halt.

From the station, they walked to their friends' house, where they were warmly received. Nevertheless, their friends were afraid to keep them in their home for too long.

At dinner, it was decided what they were going to do: Kurt was a pilot and offered to take August and his mother to a little town in Italy, close to Venice, a quick flight of approximately 50 minutes. It would be a faster way to reach their destination. From there, they would get to Venice, where they would try to take a ship to Central America. They would depart the following day after their arrival in Arnoldstein and would be at their first destination in less than an hour. They silently raised their glasses in a toast, words locked in their throats, hearts racing, feeling a strange flutter in their stomachs. In the flickering shadows of the candle lights, a hard rain lashed the windowpanes of the cozy cottage in the Alps.

In the room his friend was sharing with him, Gustl sat on the bed, staring at the rain through the window. His head propped morosely in his hands, he felt dreadful for the whole situation. Kurt tried to cheer him, coming up with different ideas. However, Gustl shuddered slightly and felt the prickle of gooseflesh. He did not want to think about the options that lay ahead of him, but he knew they were in great danger. It rained hard during good part of the night, but finally the rain subsided, thunders becoming a dying rumble.

By the time they finished breakfast the following morning, the clouds have cleared. The valley was bathed in a resplendent glow. After thanking heartily their friends, mother and son went to the field with Kurt to board the small plane.

Little did Gustl know that that short trip would be one of his nightmares for the rest of his entire life!

They took their seats and the engines started. The aircraft jolted slightly and began to move. In due time, it took off.

There were lots of clouds scattered in the sky, but they had a pretty good view of the scenery below them: neat rectangular fields, dark clumps of pine forests and a few steep red roofs.

A little while after taking off, the two passengers noted that the pilot veered the plane suddenly to the opposite direction they were heading. The aircraft pitched, shook and shuddered. The turbulence made Gustl's stomach lurch.

It didn´t take them too long wondering to realize that their plane fell prey to a German fighter aircraft.

Gustl noticed that his friend was fighting desperately not to lose control of the plane.

They had dropped through one layer of cloud; beneath them was another. Gustl was terrified. Jumping? Yes, the thought did enter his mind… However he had turned away from his own fear to try to calm down his mother. Her face was ashen and her eyes were shut tight.

"Mom, we'll be all right. Kurt knows what he is doing and in no time we'll be on firm ground."

The poor lady did not utter a word. She sat still and nodded her head, with her eyes closed tight, telling herself firmly that she was all right, that she would be all right.

He stared through the window, feeling his stomach heave and leaned back on his seat, swallowing to keep his breakfast – and his fear – down.

Unfortunately, his predictions were not to become true so quickly: they were falling fast. The pilot was fighting desperately to regain control of the aircraft; it took him all his strength to keep from diving into the ground. The plane went up and spired down like a crazy yoyo.

The two planes zoomed through the skies without stopping.

In one of the falls, Gustl felt sure he was looking death squarely in the face. He was wholly possessed in turn by doubt, fear, resignation, anger and thankfulness, because mercifully the German pilot chasing them did not act with the usual astounding German precision.

At one point, they were descending quickly. The plane swooped down, racing to what would pass for a precarious runaway. The feeble sun glinted now and then through the clouds on its wings. The plane was coming in to land; everything on the ground rushed past them. One bounce, two… they were touching down.

Chapter Seven

Somewhere in Italy

Five long hours and interminable thirty minutes after taking off, the small airplane landed in a deserted field, somewhere in Italy. Gustl thought his vision had doubled... till he realized it was because of his tears. The instant the plane taxied down to a halt, he was on his feet vowing never to get in an airplane again.

The three occupants left the airplane unsteadily, the men helping the old lady.

After making certain his friends were fine and unharmed, Kurt directed them to the closest town, to where they would have to walk. He couldn't help them any further; he had to fly back to Austria not to attract any unnecessary attention.

Before saying good-bye, Gustl asked a last favor from his friend:

"Kurt, could you deliver a letter to my fiancée, in Vienna? I wrote to her telling I would try to leave Europe and would contact her as soon as I am settled, wherever that might be."

His kind friend readily agreed to deliver the letter to Franciscka.

"I think God will reward you one day, my good friend Kurt."

Kurt looked at him and shrugged. He didn't seem convinced. Truth be told, neither was Gustl. What did he know of God and his plans?

They embraced each other and parted with tears in their eyes. They sensed it might be the last time they would be together for the rest of their lives.

It wasn't raining, but thick black clouds billowed in the sky and a cold wind blew relentlessly. Gustl shivered and felt doubts creeping in. But he clung obstinately to his hope. He stopped thinking negative thoughts and his bright eyes seemed suddenly to visualize some future in this entire ordeal. Saying encouraging words to his mother, they started walking full of purpose.

The sun cast long shadows before them, as they headed to their partly unknown destination. They climbed the lower slopes and then clambered up the last few feet. They looked over the valley spread out below and the mountains in the background. Certainly a heavenly view, were it not for the circumstances. They sat down to rest.

After a while, he helped his mother to her feet; they kept going. Night was falling fast. As they stumbled forward, darkness became impenetrable. The feeling was of icy cold vastness, terror reflected from the unseen. Crickets chirped a ragged chorus. They paused, their arms around each other, hearing nothing but the beating of their hearts. In such circumstances, one is often given some extra strength, an additional flow of adrenaline, perhaps. Soon they devised some lights where the town should be and headed towards it. Finally they got to the railway station, their feet killing them.

Both were worn-out. While his mother rested on a bench, Gustl bought tickets to the next train to Venice, which would depart at dawn, and some portions of cheese, bread and local wine to take with them in their uncertain journey.

The train came to the station some time later than the expected time of arrival. They took their seats. It departed later then the supposed time of departure. They dosed on and off. Their feet were still painful, but weariness had overcome the pain.

It must have been after two hours when the train clanked and squeaked, came to a jolt, and then was at a standstill.

Wide-eyed, they heard shouted commands as the *Guardia Secreta* stopped at each cabin to search the travellers. Some pretty rough handling by the guards as all passengers were off-loaded brought them painfully to full consciousness.

The train shed its cargo of weary civilians on to the platform of a town which was not their final destination.

Everybody was required to form a line. A stocky unshaven officer, with a battered nose, bright black eyes and black hair stood by with a clipboard writing their names on a list. A second officer held a tiny torch that moved like a glowworm in the dark. Another officer stood by, writing each name on a cardboard disc and stapling it to the clothing of each passenger. Gustl could smell the now familiar stench of sweat and fear.

The "lot", as the whole group was referred to, didn't know but they would be taken to a camp on an open truck. The unfortunates who crowded around the train and the open truck wore the blank faces of bewilderment and despair.

Chapter Eight

Every prisoner-of-war camp in Italy had a squad of *Carabinieri Reali*, the police force whose specialist efficiency preceded the advent of Fascism. These men were responsible for security, seemed to be able to over-rule the Army commandant of camps, no matter what his rank, conducted the most rigorous and unexpected searches of personal belongings, and sometimes treated prisoners with the brutality which presumably had become habitual to them in dealing with civil offenders.

The conditions in the Concentration Camps varied greatly. Some were under Italian command; others joint Italian-German command, and still others under German command. Some were Labor Camps and others Transit Camps, from which Jews were deported east. It was on one of these Transit Camps (also known as Internment Camps) that the young Silberstein and his mother were taken to.

The camp was a collection of open-air tents arrayed across a valley and surrounded by razor wire and guard towers. The prisoners were generally men suspected of resisting the Italian occupation army, or women and children who lived in villages suspected of sympathizing with the resistance, plus Jews.

"The lot" was put into a line, to wait for the officer in charge to check everybody.

When the officer arrived, he acknowledged the salutes of the sentries as they presented arms. He paused, a twisted smile crossing his sallow face. One of the guards was ordered to search each person, while he scrutinized his or her papers. Right afterwards, two burly guards with carbines would accompany the person into this barbed wire compound.

Guards slammed to attention as they accompanied mother and son to their quarters. Although is clothes were filthy, crumpled, but in some mysterious way it still held the dignity of its wearer. Gustl managed his steps with awkward dignity.

The Silbersteins were allocated a corner in one of the tents. They just looked at each other, helpless, slouched in their little cots and could not utter a single word. Tiredness and sleep took over and before long they were sleeping. One hour or so later, Gustl had a terrible nightmare and got up all of a sudden, stumbling over his suitcase, which was beside his cot. He felt himself losing control, sweat trickling down his back, his front and down his eyes. He steadied himself, avoiding falling over her mother who sat abruptly and got up terrified from her cot.

"Don't worry, mother, it was just a nightmare. Nothing happened. Let's go back to sleep."

Her eyes searched his face apprehensively; then she ran her hand lovingly over her son's damp forehead, but still did not speak a word.

He had not realized how much on edge he was. After all he still had not devised a proper way to cope with their daily lives and was not sure he would find ways to resist the Nazis and, ultimately, to survive.

Chapter Nine

Soon they found out that the area was always under surveillance; sanitation was bad; there was no organized medical care; medicines and medical equipment were scarce (the shortage was general throughout Italy); limited water and very little food (whatever food they had with them finished soon). Prisoners provided their own services which included a doctor, dentist, tailor and shoe repairer. At the far end of the camp a hut had been constructed as a drying area for washing on wet days. This hut contained heated pipes and here the prisoners would hang up their wet clothes.

The days dragged into weeks, with agonizing slowness. The nights turned cold. As they walked around the premises, their breath formed a white cloud and the wind cut through their clothes. They stamped their feet and wadded back and forth, hoping that keeping moving would keep them warmer. Sometimes it did. Most times it did not. More often than not, when they were walking past the front gates, they could hear the captain announcing:

"Twenty prisoners more."

The man in charge of the inspection would get a letter. The head gate guard would offer a brusque nod and the newcomers would march in. Mother and son could not help feeling their guts get cold and colder, as they watched unhappy people arrive at the prison yard, deprived of all their freedom, their privacy and their poise.

Wordlessly, they would go back to their quarters, half-expecting to get acquainted to those sad people arriving at the camp, who were too immersed in their own misery to speak or too afraid of sharing their fate with strangers.

Life did not get any better. Disease spread more quickly and they did their best to keep their things and themselves as clean as possible. They had to rise at six AM and had plain coffee. Parade and counted at seven. For breakfast, they got a cup of thin gruel. Tea made from Red Cross parcels at twelve and a slice of bread at one. For dinner, a soup so watered down that the grains of rice could be counted.

Every time they got their horrible food, Gustl couldn't help himself remembering the nice meals they shared as a happy family, around the gleaming walnut table with its place-settings of fine china, crystal, and crested silver cutlery.

At the end of each day, there was a roll call, where Italian soldiers would yell:

"Tutti fuori, anche morti!" (Everyone out, including the dead!)

While the treatment of prisoners by the Italian Army or by the *Carabinieri Reali* was sometimes harsh, ordinary Italians were often prepared to go out of their way to do prisoners of war a good turn without any hope of reward. Women threw bread into camps and prisoners who gave their water bottles to civilians to be filled with water had them returned full of wine. The machine of Fascism regarded it as a duty to behave oppressively, although this was not the sentiment of most Italians.

Like many of the Italian camps, this one had beautiful surroundings, including a view of the distant Dolomite Mountains. However, the weather – gray and humid, with rain drizzling down almost continuously – did nothing to improve the prisoners' spirits.

But Gustl was a very nice-going person, talkative and friendly. He always had a joke or a fun story to tell even to the soldiers. He found a way to get to the camp kitchen, where he started to bake chocolate cakes, very much appreciated by the high rank soldiers. His mother offered to bake apple pies and soon both got to live a lighter life in the camp.

As both spoke fluent Italian, they became friends to an Italian priest who called on the camp regularly. One day, he offered the Silbersteins the chance to immigrate to Brazil. Both agreed promptly. It was not what Gustl had planned, but after all, Central America or South America would probably be the same thing.

Chapter Ten

The prospect of leaving the camp and being able to be free again made them wait for their papers anxiously.

After a few days the priest came back with bad news:

"I am sorry, August, but I could not get the papers for you."

When he looked baffled the priest hastened to explain:

"Brazilian Jewish quota is over."

Under the semi fascist President Getúlio Vargas' regime (1930–1945), the Ministry of Foreign Affairs distributed a secret memo urging all Brazilian consuls not to grant visas to Jews. Immigration restrictions and the activities of a fascist party generated an environment of nationalistic xenophobia.

Thousands of immigrants from Nazi-dominated Europe were barred. Restrictions limiting the immigration of Jews were instituted using economic, political, racial, and religious selectivity to prevent "too many" Jews from joining Latin American Catholic society and from competing with local merchants, workers, professionals, and entrepreneurs. Jewish immigration was severely curtailed and almost illegal.

Apparently, the Silbersteins were included in this situation.

"Troubles, troubles, always troubles!" – Said Mrs. Silberstein mournfully.

Gustl was left shaky and depressed and his mind reacted slowly to everything. He was fed up to the teeth of living in such conditions.

He went to his cot, sat down and looked thoughtful. His heart had missed a beat, a dead weight seemed to have hit him in the stomach and a dull pain struck him across the chest. The news had been shattering to him. He spent a sleepless night, twisting and turning and couldn't help stop wondering what the outcome of their situation would be. He and his mother were devastated with the news, but could do nothing about it.

Life went on in the camp, till the priest's next visit, when he came with a solution to their problem, offering another opportunity to leave Europe: he would baptize them. As Catholics, both would get permits to live in Brazil.

And that is exactly what they did: August got an Italian name to add to his name. From then on his name would be August Pietro Silberstein. Before that, like every Jew, his papers bore the brand name Israel: August **Israel** Silberstein.

"Now, August, I am sure you are happy!" – Asserted the priest cheerfully.

"Well…" – answered Gustl – "that is a statement of the obvious if ever there was one!"

Thanks to this Italian priest, Gustl and Clothilde got a piece of paper with a stamp on it that made the difference between life and death. With papers in hand, knowing they would be able to manage breaching immigration barriers, they had a nice feeling of happiness, and experienced a brief peace in the turmoil times they were living, being able to depart the camp quickly.

Like many other Europeans fleeing from Hitler's wrath, the Silbersteins made spectacular and audacious efforts in order to overcome the unending obstacles imposed upon them.

Chapter Eleven

Those intervening weeks passed by as a chaotic blur. Finally the Silbersteins were able to board a ship that would take them away from Europe for an uncertain future, although probably much better than the one they would have if remaining in Austria or even Italy.

Mrs. Silberstein thought it was too cold to stay on the upper deck when the ship set sail; she chose to go to the cabin. Her son stayed a little bit outside, staring at the shading of the ocean waters and at the receding skyline of the European land. Someone close by said aloud what he had been thinking:

"Say good-bye to Europe!"

Sadly, Gustl went to the bar. He got some brandy, hoping it would help him sleep better, knowing it wouldn't. He drank it slowly, thinking of the life he left behind, of his fiancée, his business, his friends. He swallowed the rest of his brandy.

"May I join you?" - asked a young woman holding a glass of champagne, interrupting Gustl's gloomy reflections.

He looked startled at the pretty face beside him. He'd instantly seen the appeal of the woman getting ready to introduce herself. Tall, pale-skinned, blue-eyed, curvy, beautiful hair, so fair it was almost white, tumbling past her shoulders.

"Of course!"

"Why such a gloom face?"

"Well, I think I am fighting the urge to jump in the sea…"

"And swim back to Hitler's arms?"

He gave a hollow laugh.

"You're right. I have to put these thoughts out of my mind before I am insane. But you see, exhaustion and brandy sent my turbulent worries soaring to new heights. My mind began to work furiously, coming up with new problems and unsolved solutions, which I cannot share with my worn-out mother, nor with my fiancée."

"Why not?" – She asked, and waited for his answer taking a long sip of the sparkling beverage.

"My mother is worn-out after all we've been through."

"And your fiancée?"

The half-smile on August's face faded, but he did not evade the question. After a short hesitation, he said bluntly:

"She stayed in Europe."

"Then you may share your problems and worries with me!"

"How can I possibly share my problems with a stranger?"

She rested her champagne glass on the bar top and offered a handshake:

"Hello! I'm Sophie Engel. Nice to meet you!"

"My pleasure. August Silberstein."

"So, you left your fiancée home and are going to explore the Americas all by yourself? I mean, with your mother?"

"It is not that simple."

"Nothing is simple in life. Where are you from?"

"From Vienna. And you?"

"From Salzburg. Which part of Brazil have you chosen and what will you be doing there?"

"I don't know yet. We'll arrive in Santos and I will look for a job as a Pharmacist. What about you?"

"My parents have some farms in the south of Brazil. And that's where I am supposed to go. At least, till the situation is better in Europe, to where I intend to come back as quickly as possible."

"It looks like you are not too thrilled to live in a tropical country!"

"No, I am not. Brazilians are very nice, mind you. However… besides São Paulo and Rio, the cities are very quiet for my taste. No operas, no galas… And the language… oh, my God! Portuguese is so difficult."

"Then why did you come?"

"I had just broken off with my fiancé. My parents are not too comfortable leaving me alone to fend for myself in such uncertain times and as I refused to come down the Equator, they stopped sending me money. I had no other options."

"Now that you know about me… what about you?"

Reaching into his pocket, August pulled a pack of cigarettes, offered her and took one for him. He lit them and as he drew on his cigarette, he mused about Franciscka. It was incredible how much this young woman reminded him of her. At least physically. He sighed, roused himself from these ruminations and gave his undivided attention to the gorgeous girl next to him.

They spent hours talking. Then, they said good-night, promising to have breakfast together on the following day.

Chapter Twelve

Gustl went to his cabin but could not go to sleep.

The image of Franciscka and his recent friend Sophie did not leave his mind.

It was dawn when he leaned back in the uncomfortable chair he was sitting, incredibly weary and completely beaten. Sunlight peeped through the porthole. The golden wash from the sun created shadows on the wall that looked eerily like the phantoms of the future that were in his mind.

Still he did not feel up to go to his berth and sleep.

He took a piece of paper and his fountain pen and started writing to his fiancée.

In the long letter, he told Franciscka he did not have the faintest idea what he would be able to do in a land where he did not speak the language nor had any idea of its custom. However, he imagined worst things which could have happened to him and his mother in their country: persecuted, maybe failing to survive persecution, caught, even prisoned! The thought that seeking refuge abroad was the wisest decision he could have chosen, made he feel better and he hoped made her feel better too. He declared his love to her and put the letter in an envelope. He would mail this letter, together with all the others he intended to write to her, as soon as they reached their destination.

He glanced at his watch and thought that it would take ages for the ship to reach Brazil. In a way… it did.

From the moment they left the European port until the outline of Brazilian land loomed on the horizon, he and his mother spent restless days, not only worried about their future, but also afraid of what might happen during the sea travel: possible German submarine force attacks (their powerful U-boats proved to be formidable foes, and a very real threat), or severe health problem during the long trip. Besides, this journey could also be hazardous because of the weather. They could not leave worries behind, like they left their home, their life, their homeland.

The crew did their best to make life on board as agreeable as possible, in spite of the war hardships. If the weather was fine, passengers were invited to take some fresh air on the upper deck. Almost every day mother and son watched silently in awe the sunset, feeling like their lives were like the red sun, evaporating so quickly on the horizon, disappearing into a sea of interlaced clouds. Usually they dined with others in the Grand Dining Room, realizing what a diverse lot their traveling companions were.

However, young Gustl (now feeling very old) knew in his guts that he would have very few happy memories of the time and was sure he would not be able to tell too many details of this trip, because during it, half of him was dead.

He would nonetheless vividly recall a terrible storm in the middle of the trip that almost blew the ship out of the water. The storm hit with gale-force winds churning sky and sea. The ship was struck many times by towering waves, and tossed like a matchstick in the ocean. An experience he would describe as "sheer unmitigated Hell".

Chapter Thirteen

Sophie was a breath of fresh air in the pharmacist's turbulent world. Undoubtedly pretty, she was exuberant, teasing, boisterous, and full of fun. They found many things in common besides sharing the same motherland and talked for hours on end; this turned the journey into something much more pleasant than both expected. They made all the meals together and stayed together the whole day and good part of the evenings.

A few days before the end of the trip, the Capitan organized a ball after dinner. The dance floor was swirling with the patterns of Viennese Waltzes, while people around it laughed, chattered and stared. As far as everybody in the ballroom was concerned, there was no threat of war at all.

Gustl invited Sophie to dance. He put his arm around her, and then winced when she just sort of melted against him. She pressed herself even closer to him, wanting to be nearer and nearer. Gustl drew in a shaky breath, staring at her. In a split-second glance he noticed that she might be in love with him. Activity surrounding them faded, it was as if they were alone in the universe. He almost kissed her, but reason took hold of him. He stopped dancing and said with his throat tight with tension:

"Come on! Let's go outside to breathe some fresh air!"

Gradually the cacophony of the ball faded and they could hear only the swish of the waves on the upper deck. The sea air was fresh with the tang of salt on the breeze, which played with her hair, whipping it around her face. She reached up to pull it back, brushing back the strands with tremulous fingers.

"Sophie, you are very attractive and charming," - he said, glancing over the water – "however, I have a fiancée who I intend to marry."

Her mouth tightened. She blinked and stared at him. He stared back. At those tears and at her face, too. His hazel eyes, narrowed with concern, looked deep into hers.

She turned away from him, grabbed on the railing to steady herself and gave him a tentative sideway smile, nodding at him.

"Of course!" – She mumbled as her shoulders dropped.

"I am sorry."

"Don't be!" – And she gave him a skeptical look.

Gustl was instantly sad because he got a glimpse of the pain beneath her façade, but he could do nothing about it.

"Let's just be good friends."

"Forget it! It won't happen."

And she fled the deck, down to her own cabin. It was the last time they saw each other. Sophie refused to see him, did not answer him when he knocked at her door, and ignored the notes he scribbled and shoved under it.

When European shore was just a memory, the ship finally docked at the Port of Santos, after a month on the sea. The Silbersteins felt elated at arriving safe and sound in Brazil, an accomplishment that let them and most of the passengers feel a delicious sense of freedom.

The ship anchored in a not at all balmy day; the newly arrived walked down the gangway with certain uneasiness, and descended into the midst of many freighters waiting to be loaded with coffee beans.

As they stepped out of the ship, in a very uncomfortable heat, Gustl felt unchanged but he knew that his life was going to be different from any existence he had ever dreamed for himself. He expected to see Sophie once again, but she waited for everybody to leave the ship. Only then did she leave her quarters and made her way through her new homeland all by herself.

Chapter Fourteen

Santos – Brazil

To some, a tropical country epitomizes the steamiest of adventures. However, for Clothilde, the possible white sand, exotic beaches and tangled inhospitable jungle meant mainly one nuisance after the other.

They were apprehensive to go through customs, but the officials, who spoke no German at all, did not create any difficulties for them to enter Brazilian soil.

After getting their two pieces of luggage, they got a cab and went to a hotel. From the window of their room they could see the beach, a huge stretch of sand, to where, by the way, during their stay in town, the Silbersteins went only once: both got sunburned after staying for a short period of time by the seaside. Feeling very uncomfortable after that, they did not want to go through the experience again.

Santos was a cheerful enough seaside town, with shops bulging with buckets and spades, beach balls in every color of the rainbow and – of course – the latest bathing costumes, each year more daring than the previous one.

Their first day in town was going to be exactly like the following ones.

It was early morning. The sun was shining brilliantly. The air was already vibrating with intense heat. The sea salt fragrance lingered in the air. Gustl could fathom what the rest of the day would be like. Every day he went around town trying to find a job he could perform. Lack of knowledge of Portuguese proved to be a big obstacle.

He did not find anybody speaking German, although he could communicate in Italian. He went from one place to the other, coming back to the hotel without anything to give him hope of getting established or of finding conditions for practicing his profession in Santos. At the end of each day, he was drenched with perspiration, tired from the heat and footsore. At a certain point, he thought he was prepared to take a job that would be beneath his qualifications and work experience, but not even that did he come across.

Used to the bustle of a metropolis like Vienna, the Silbersteins were not too excited to stay in a little town that was a hundred years old and had just in the beginning of that year risen to the category of City. Besides, there seemed to be no work possibilities for the young pharmacist, who could not speak more than a few words of Portuguese.

They were distraught and unhappy.

After a few days suffering with the heat and not finding any work, Gustl decided that Santos was not for them. He'd rather try his luck in São Paulo.

Chapter Fifteen

São Paulo – Brazil

The Silbersteins drove up a winding driveway which made the connection between Santos and the São Paulo region. They were enthralled with the breathtaking views of majestic green mountains mingling with the sea down below. Banks of tropical flowers helped produce stunning views.

In São Paulo, they checked in a Hotel downtown.

One day, Gustl met in a very busy street an old acquaintance.

"Fritz?"

"August?"

"I can't believe we should meet here, so far away from home!"

"Isn't it a most extraordinary coincidence?" – Gustl greeted warmly Fritz Klein, who was accompanied by a young woman.

"August, this is my girlfriend, Vera Bosányi. Vera, this is my old classmate August Silberstein, from Vienna."

"How do you do?" – Gustl turned and looked at Vera, an inexplicable smile seeping over his face, as he surveyed her from head to foot. She had gorgeous eyes, long, sooty lashes and beautiful hands adorned with slender fingers. He stared at her with intensity, not even bothering to conceal his curiosity and interest in the beautiful young woman.

The pharmacist's manners were impeccable, showing the gallantry of a good upbringing. He greeted her with a polite kiss on the hand. She felt herself blush beneath his amused gaze but answered with admirable calm:

"Nice to meet you!" – She replied, as she noted the modern, daring and sophisticated man, who certainly doted on perfume; she could perceive a unique aromatic woody fragrance, decidedly masculine: a seductive man with a forceful and passionate character.

"Nice to meet you, too!" – He replied, as he grasped her hand in a firm grip.

His eyes twinkled at the sight of Vera. Their glances locked. They continued to stare at each other, their hands still clasped. His scrutiny was intense and she knew he was taken with her as she was with him.

Vera was experiencing an overwhelming and spontaneous attraction to him. She had to force herself to let his hand go.

"When have you arrived?"

"Last week. With my mother. We are in a hotel close by and I have to find a job."

"So, August, couldn't face your military duties, did not want to fight for our country and decided to come to Brazil?" – Fritz added a little too pompously, laughing. He looked at his companion, waiting for her to follow suite.

Apparently he thought the remark was funny; however, she didn't see the humor at all.

For a split second, Gustl just gaped, mouth dropping open. He looked uncomfortable, tugging at the collar and tie that suddenly started to strangle him.

"No. I came to Brazil for other reasons. We had some problems in Vienna." – He replied tersely, the smile vanishing form his face.

"Well, I am sure the legal authorities there would have solved your problems if you had insisted."

Gustl hesitated as if mustering the following words to suit the situation.

"German authorities" – he contradicted scornfully, frowning at the old "friend" – "couldn't care less. Besides, with Hitler taking over I don't think we would have our country the way we would like to."

"I can't stand that Hitler character: what a braggart and bully! Disgraceful the way he overran Austria. That man is nothing but a thug."

He listened to the outburst in silence. Obviously the young woman did not like the Nazis. He found her enchanting. She spoke fluent German and he soon found out that she spoke equally flawless Portuguese and Hungarian as well.

"Vera!" – Fritz exclaimed quite in awe of her tone. – "Is that a way to speak?"

Vera knitted her eyebrows disapprovingly at his remark. Gustl decided to change the unwelcome subject.

"Anyway, now that I am here, I need to find a teacher to learn Portuguese."

"I am a teacher!" – The young woman interposed.

"No kidding? And would you have time to teach me and my mother?"

No doubt delighted that she might be able to see this attractive man again, Vera readily agreed to start teaching him Portuguese lessons right away.

"Of course! Where are you staying?"

Gustle's spirits soared crazily, simply because she agreed to teach him Portuguese, while watching delighted a heated blush stain her smooth cheeks.

"At Hotel República, a few blocks from here. When could you come?"

"How about Friday morning, at 10 o'clock?"

"Perfect! Very nice seeing you, Fritz. Good-bye!" – He went about his way with the beginning of wishful hope warming him.

Fritz wasn't so sure it was nice meeting this old acquaintance of his in São Paulo.

Chapter Sixteen

Mrs. Silberstein seemed to like the Portuguese teacher a lot. Besides, she was very glad to be able to speak to an intelligent woman in her own language.

The older woman used to carry on poignant conversations, reminiscing the time she lived in Europe, their long and tiring trip to Brazil, and how she missed everything and everyone there. When this happened, usually after the class, while they were sipping coffee, Vera would hold the old woman's hands while she talked about people who had left footprints on her memory when they had walked across her life. When Mrs. Silberstein was through, she gazed thoughtfully at her coffee cup for a long time. Sometimes she sobbed. Vera understood the old woman's mood, the necessity of these outbursts and just sat there, supportive, quiet, waiting for the sobs to subdue.

After a few classes, August insisted on accompanying his teacher wherever she would be heading.

"Let's have some coffee somewhere."

"I'm sorry; I have other classes to give and some errands to run."

"Ah, could you deny me a few more minutes with the most beautiful, intelligent and witty teacher I could ever think of having?"

"Have you always been so gallant?" – She asked.

"It's one of my most attractive qualities!" – He replied smoothly.

She rolled her eyes at him in laughing exasperation, but when he continued to regard her in waiting silence, she gave in and let him accompany her to her next student's house. It was not too far away from his hotel; they should have taken a tram, however they decided to walk. And walk they did, laughing a lot at the things each other said. Sooner than they expected, they got to their destination.

He waited outside the house till she finished her class.

"Ok! Now we can have some coffee." – She said happily.

"I think we'd better have some ice-cream. I thought I would die here in this heat. Thankfully, this tree has a nice shadow, or you would have found just a puddle of sweat waiting for you!"

She smiled at his contagious humor.

There were some nice Cafés spread in the downtown area, so it was not difficult at all to find one. He chose a nice spot by a window and asked for their ice-creams and coffee.

Chapter Seventeen

He didn't notice how but suddenly he was telling her about the dangerous trip from Austria till he got to Brazil, step by step.

Sometimes he would stop abruptly, in the middle of a sentence, and Vera was not sure whether he was reluctant to tell her that particular passage or whether his memory momentarily failed him.

Unaware of the time, the young woman stared at Gustl, silent, stunned and also flattered that he was telling such personal facts to her. She was listening to him with an expression of such rapt fascination that now and then a smile tugged at his lips.

As if releasing pent-ups reminiscence, among other things, he told her how he had feared his Jewishness.

"But now, how do you feel about it?"

He waved her question into thin air.

"The Nazis are dedicated to eliminating the Jews. Now that I have been baptized as a Catholic, and intend to make my home here, on the other side of the Atlantic, I do hope this Jewishness of mine is of little consequence."

He reached for his coffee, which by then was cold and tasting awful, but tossed it down, as if he were trying to wash away the taste of his words, the taste of bad memories, then he stared absently into the empty cup.

She looked grave when he wearily came to the end of his hotchpotch of survival scraps. She drew a long breath and there was a gleam of tears in her eyes. With a slight shudder, she said:

"Oh, my God, the courage you must have had to go through all that, even more so having your mother with you, trying to protect her, to lessen her sufferings, her doubts…"

He nodded silent approval at her acuity. He was a little astonished – and impressed – that she arrived at that conclusion with such quick ease, because he did not exaggerate facts on telling the whole story.

They spoke for a while of the terrible things that were happening in Germany and in Europe in general, shaking their heads sadly.

"It is that megalomaniac Hitler! He is the one who gives all the orders. The German army is in complete control. They pull the strings and the puppets have to dance for him. A deplorable situation."

"Can't people not realize that Hitler is telling lies every time he promises a thousand years of peace?"

Hypnotized by her face, he decided to say something to break the tension of the subject and the spell he felt just looking at her.

"Apparently, there are many people who think like our brave Fritz, who is safe here and doubts other people's reason for not fighting for what he considers to be HIS country. Actually, I think he would be glad to lead a squadron of bombing planes which would indiscriminately drop bombs if the German legal authorities would have ordered. Or do whatever German authorities would have ordered. Although that hardly amounts to bravery!"

It was a small joke, but she giggled, breaking the tension. He watched her eye shimmer with amusement.

They kept exchanging ideas as the afternoon advanced and people passed to and fro in front of the café they were sitting at. That is when Vera told him she also came from Europe fleeing from the war, but in better conditions than him and his mother.

"Maybe you came using the same ship I did. Which ship did you take?"

She blushed and answered:

"This is not important. What matters is that that ship was the only hope I had to leave Europe, as it was the last one that left the continent before the war broke."

Chapter Eighteen

"What about dinner tonight?" – Gustl asked Vera after the class was over and Mrs. Silberstein has left the room.

"I can't." – Vera said. – "I have other classes to give."

"And tomorrow?"

"I give classes till late tomorrow and Thursday as well, till late."

"What about Friday?"

"That sounds nice." – Vera felt a pull of attraction she tried to ignore. – "Is your mother coming too?"

"Why would I want her to come too?"

"I am beginning to feel" – Mrs. Silberstein laughingly remarked from the doorway – "quite horribly unwanted around here!"

At the sound of his mother's voice, Gustl tipped his head back, closed his eyes and hastily invented an excuse for his tactlessness.

"Sorry, Mother, but I thought you would be too tired at night to go out, as you usually prefer to have dinner here at the hotel!"

She winked at her son and said:

"You are completely right about that. It is better that you two go out and have dinner in a nice restaurant somewhere. I'll have dinner here at the hotel, as usual."

Mrs. Silberstein was very glad to notice that her son was in much better spirits after they had started Portuguese classes. And she was sure it was not because of learning the language he was so happy. She had given a great thought about Gustl's fiancée and wasn't sure the girl would risk coming to an unknown place like Brazil even if she really loved her son. She has also noticed right after they have arrived, every night he would devote some time to write long letters to Franciscka and would mail them in the morning. As far as she knew no letters have arrived for him; he has written less and less.

"It's better that you two go by yourselves."

"Ok, Mother! So, Vera, Friday, then?"

The Portuguese teacher presented him with a winsome smile and nodded emphatically:

"As you know, Fritz is a pianist of relative success in South America and sometimes he goes on tour for some concerts. This Friday he is off on a tour, so I think I can have dinner with you."

Chapter Nineteen

The sun had not dropped below the horizon, yet. August felt restless and nervous like a schoolboy. He didn't know why. After all, he was just having dinner with a nice Portuguese teacher who, by the way, was an old friend's girlfriend.

He arrived at the rendezvous half an hour earlier, tingling with excitement – and a touch of apprehension at the unknown future ahead.

He sat at a table where he could see Vera arriving. While he waited, he could think of nothing but Vera. He did try to avoid that and forced himself to focus on his fiancée's face. However, his thoughts veered back to the Portuguese teacher. Suddenly he was brimming with feelings he didn't fully understand. Or did **not** want to understand. He liked being with her, enjoyed her wry sense of humor, her easygoing way and her brightness. He knew she didn't expect anything from him, except long and agreeable talks. And that is exactly what he was able to give her and what she would have.

Presently he saw her approaching the restaurant. She had seemed ravishing from a distance and she was just as striking close to. Not conventionally beautiful, perhaps, but her face was so extraordinary. She moved in a graceful, upright manner, which carried the calm breath of confidence. She saw him, waved and came to meet him at his table. Politely, he rose to greet her and help her sit at the chair. Dinner was ordered and they talked about thousands of issues. Among them, of course, the war.

"The war situation is still looking pretty grim;" – he lowered his voice as he looked across the table at her – "more and more Jews are seeking shelter from the persecution and" – his voice fell to a whisper – "more new anti-Jewish laws have been passed, forbidding Jewish music and books!" – He spread his hands.

Again Vera gave her views on the subject, telling him about things she got to know through letters that she received from some members of her family that lived in Hungary.

Gustl absorbed every word she'd said.

They were having coffee when a shadow interposed itself between them. Both looked up at the same time to find Fritz standing beside them. He walked around the table, came to Vera's side and laid his long-fingered hands on her shoulders. She flinched and ducked out from under his touch.

"So, is this where you give classes now?"

"Oh, hallo, Fritz!" – greeted August.

Fritz's cheeks muscles tightened as he clenched his jaw; he looked contemptuously at his opponent's outstretched hand.

Vera met her boyfriend's icy gaze squarely; feeling slightly irritable with the innuendo on his question, she could not resist saying:

"No, Fritz. This is where I came to have dinner with my student. Weren't you supposed to be in a tour?"

"Yes, indeed. But we had some problems with the agent and had to call it off. I had a last minute appointment with the new agent in this restaurant and look what I find!"

"What you find is exactly what you see: a teacher and a student having dinner in a restaurant."

"I don't think so!" – Fritz's eyes narrowed; he clinched his hands into fists and banged them on the table.

August and Vera stood up instantaneously. As Vera watched her boyfriend, all she could think was that he was far outclassed in what she perceived now to be a silently furious competition between the two men. He radiated anger and hate of August in heavy waves that seemed to swim through the room, making the air almost too thick to breath.

"Strange that you might say that because there is nothing wrong going on." – replied August, his face clouding. He had the distinct feeling that the other guy was exerting every ounce of his control to keep his emotions in check.

"I think we'd better go home now!" – He ordered Vera, who felt a threat in his voice, implied, if not stated. – "And you, August, mark my words: Don't you ever get close to my girlfriend again!"

Momentarily undone by this surge of unprecedented emotion, August had been incapable of uttering a single word and fumed silently.

Vera had the feeling that the guy has never hated another human being as much in his life. If her legs hadn't felt like overcooked spaghetti, she might have walked away from the scene all by herself. Her heart was galloping in her chest and her stomach kept twisting, as if a giant, unseen fist was squeezing at it mercilessly. Could this get any worse? Her head ached and the tumult in her stomach stepped up a notch.

The couple left the restaurant hurriedly, he guiding her purposefully towards the door. She accompanied him meekly and didn't say a word to August, who paid the bill but stayed for a long time sitting there, smoking one cigarette after the other, thinking about everything that happened that evening. Later on, he left forlornly to his hotel, chewing his rage.

On the way, he felt a burst of sudden loneliness, an uncomfortable awareness that all the warmth, friendship… and love vanished into thin air. Love? How come?

Chapter Twenty

Now that he thought about it… Since he started having Portuguese classes he stopped writing to his fiancée. Presently he got to a very uncomfortable conclusion: he realized he was in love with Vera. He in love with whom? Vera? How ridiculous! His fiancée was Franciscka!

August's heart stuttered a little, but he swallowed hard and pulled in a deep breath. He couldn't really believe this was happening, but it was hard to avoid the truth.

What was he going to do now? After all, his ex-friend was right. Something must have been in the air between him and Vera. Was she in love with him?

With all these questions bubbling in his mind, he arrived at his hotel. There, in the foyer a tear stricken faced Vera was waiting for him.

"Vera, what happened?"

She shook her head and through the tears managed to say miserably:

"I cannot stand my boyfriend anymore. We have lived together for almost a year, but tonight he threatened me and was on the verge of losing control when I decided to run away. I have no family in São Paulo. Therefore, I have nowhere to go."

He held her in her arms as she wept nonstop. When she calmed down a little, he caressed her cheek lightly. It was velvety to the touch and infinitely smooth. His heart seemed to lunge for his ribs. Then, he asked her:

"Vera, would you move in with me? We'll rent an apartment and start a life together." – There was such an earnest plea in his eyes, and his expression was so loving, that she felt her breath catching in her throat.

She clutched his hands, peered up at him. Anxiously, he looked down at her face, tears of happiness glistening on her eyes. Probably the world went on in its timeless way while they kissed for the first time.

"Come on, let's go for a walk. Both of us need fresh air and I think it is a good idea to have that unfinished coffee we left untouched at the restaurant."

He gave her his hand and they remained linked as they started to walk in silence the few yards till the beautiful Square across the hotel. It was a clear spring evening. Some of the trees were still bare. On these, a fuzz of new leaves blurred their outline against the street lamps. The park was almost empty: the small stretch of lawn ending in the waters of the pond, still and gleaming in the moonlight.

"I have to tell you something, Gustl."

"What is it?"

"Remember you asked me the name of the ship I took, when I fled Europe?"

"Yes, I remember. And thought it was quite strange you did not tell me its name."

"That ship was my ticket to a safe and hopeful happy future life. And so are you. The name of the ship was Augustus!"

He nodded, his expressive features glowing with delight.

"I love you, my dear Mrs. Silberstein to be."

"I love you too, my dear husband to be."

He held her cheeks in both his hands and kissed her tenderly on the lips, as though sealing a promise of undying love.

Printed by Amazon Italia Logistica S.r.l.
Torrazza Piemonte (TO), Italy

48168088R00045